52-WEEK

DEVOTIONAL

FOR KIDS

Published by Midsummer Bloom Books

First Edition: September 2025
Printed in the United States of America

Contents

Welcome

Hey there! We're so glad you're here. This devotional is your weekly guide to growing closer to God in a fun, simple, and practical way. Each week you'll read a short Bible verse, learn a big idea that connects to a story from the Bible, think about how it fits your life, and try a challenge to put it into action.

This book is for kids just like you—curious, brave, and ready to learn. Whether you love sports, art, science, music, or just hanging out with friends, God cares about every part of your life. He's with you at school, at home, on the bus, at the game, and even when you're brushing your teeth!

Here's how each week works:

> » Bible Verse: A short verse to remember.

> » The Big Idea: What the verse means and a Bible story to bring it to life.

> » Let's Think About It: Questions to help you reflect.

> » A Simple Prayer: A quick prayer you can say to God.

> » Your Weekly Challenge: A fun step to live out what you learned.

Are you ready? Let's go on this adventure with God—one week at a time!

Week 1: Wonderfully Made

Bible Verse

"I praise you, for I am fearfully and wonderfully made." — Psalm 139:14 (ESV)

The Big Idea

Do you ever look in the mirror and notice all the little things that make you, you—your smile, your freckles, your hair, your laugh? The Bible tells us that God made you on purpose and with love. King David wrote Psalm 139 to say that God knows us completely—when we sit, when we stand, and even what we're going to say before we say it!

Think about the first chapter of the Bible. God made everything—light, oceans, trees, stars, animals—and called it good. But when He made people, He did something extra special: He made us in His image. That means you are designed to reflect who God is by showing love, kindness, creativity, and courage.

Sometimes kids compare themselves to others: "She runs faster," or "He draws better." But God didn't make a copy—He made an original. You! When you use the gifts God gave you, you shine. Whether you're helping a friend, solving a tough problem, or making something beautiful, you're showing the world a bit of what God is like.

So remember: you're not an accident, you're a masterpiece. God made you wonderfully—and He doesn't make mistakes.

Let's Think About It

» What's one special gift or talent God has given you?

» How can you use that gift to help someone this week?

A Simple Prayer

Dear God, thank You for making me wonderfully. Help me to see myself the way You see me. Amen.

Your Weekly Challenge

Make a "God-made-me" list of five things you like about how God made you—skills, traits, or interests—and thank Him for each one.

Week 2: Brave in the Den

Bible Verse

"When I am afraid, I put my trust in you." — Psalm 56:3 (ESV)

The Big Idea

Have you ever felt nervous about a presentation or worried about a big game? Daniel knew what fear felt like—he was thrown into a den full of hungry lions! Why? Because he kept praying to God even when a law said he shouldn't. Daniel wasn't brave because he was super strong; he was brave because he trusted God.

All night long, Daniel stayed in the den—but he wasn't alone. God sent an angel to shut the lions' mouths. In the morning, the king rushed to see if Daniel was okay. He was! Daniel's courage reminded everyone that God is powerful and worthy of trust.

Being brave doesn't mean you never feel afraid. It means that when fear shows up, you run to God, not away. You can whisper a prayer before a test, ask God for help when you're lonely, or trust Him when you need to do the right thing. God is with you in classrooms, on playgrounds, and yes—even in "lion's dens" like tough situations that feel scary.

God is bigger than your fears, and He's right there with you.

Let's Think About It

» What's something that makes you feel afraid?

» What's a short prayer you can say when fear shows up?

A Simple Prayer

God, when I'm scared, help me trust You like Daniel did. Thank You for staying with me. Amen.

Your Weekly Challenge

Choose one scary-but-good thing to do this week—like raising your hand or sitting with someone new—and do it while saying, "God, I trust You."

Week 3: Trust the Map

Bible Verse

"Trust in the LORD with all your heart."
— Proverbs 3:5 (ESV)

The Big Idea

Imagine you're on a hike with a map. You come to a fork in the trail. One path looks fun and easy; the other looks steep and tough. Which do you choose? Sometimes life feels like that. We have choices every day—friends, words, attitudes—and not all paths are good ones.

Abraham had to trust God's "map." God told him to leave his home and go to a land he'd never seen. That's a big deal! Abraham didn't know every step, but he trusted the One who did. Trusting God means believing that His way is best, even when we don't understand the whole plan.

How do we follow God's map? We read His Word, pray for wisdom, listen to wise people, and ask, "What would please God?" It's like checking the trail markers along the way. When we lean on God—not just our own ideas—He helps us choose what's right and keeps us from getting lost.

God's map is trustworthy. He knows the path, and He walks it with you.

Let's Think About It

» What's a decision you need to make this week?

» How can you ask God for help to choose wisely?

A Simple Prayer

Lord, help me trust Your way with all my heart. Lead me step by step. Amen.

Your Weekly Challenge

Before bed each night, ask God to guide one choice you'll face tomorrow—and look for His help.

Week 4: Be a Kind Neighbor

Bible Verse

"Be kind to one another, tenderhearted,"
— Ephesians 4:32 (ESV)

The Big Idea

Have you ever seen someone sitting alone at lunch or struggling with their books? Jesus told a story about a man who was hurt on the side of the road. Two people walked past him, but one person—a Samaritan—stopped to help. He bandaged the man's wounds, gave him a ride, and made sure he was safe. That's kindness in action!

Being kind isn't just feeling sorry; it's doing something to help. Kindness looks like sharing your snack, inviting someone into the game, or using gentle words when you're frustrated. It also means being "tenderhearted"—caring about how others feel, even if they're different from you.

God was kind to us first. Jesus came to rescue us when we needed help the most. When we remember

His kindness, it becomes easier to pass it on. Kindness might seem small, but it changes classrooms, families, and friendships—one kind act at a time.

You can be the person who stops to help. That's what a good neighbor does.

Let's Think About It

» Who needs kindness from you this week?

» What's one small action you can take today?

A Simple Prayer

Jesus, thank You for Your kindness to me. Help me be a good neighbor who shows love. Amen.

Your Weekly Challenge

Do three secret acts of kindness this week. Don't brag—let God see, and enjoy the joy of helping!

Week 5: Talk to God Anytime

Bible Verse

"pray without ceasing" — 1 Thessalonians 5:17 (ESV)

The Big Idea

What if you could text God anytime? Guess what—you can talk to Him anytime through prayer! Prayer doesn't need fancy words or a special place. It's simply talking and listening to God about everything: your joys, worries, questions, and plans.

Daniel prayed three times a day—even when it got him in trouble. Jesus prayed early in the morning and before important decisions. The Bible shows us that prayer is powerful, not because we're perfect at it, but because God listens.

You can pray when you wake up, before a quiz, when a friend is hurting, or when you're thankful for pizza night. Try telling God: "Sorry" for wrong choices, "Thank You" for good gifts, and "Please" for help.

You can also be quiet and listen—God can guide your thoughts through His Word and His peace.

Prayer is like breathing for your soul—regular, natural, and life-giving.

Let's Think About It

» When is your favorite time to pray?

» What is one thing you want to start talking to God about?

A Simple Prayer

God, thank You for always listening. Help me talk to You through my day and hear Your guidance. Amen.

Your Weekly Challenge

Set three "prayer moments" each day—morning, lunchtime, and bedtime. Keep it simple and real.

Week 6: Let It Go

Bible Verse

"forgiving one another, as the Lord has forgiven you," — Colossians 3:13 (ESV)

The Big Idea

Have you ever had a friend say something that hurt your feelings? Holding onto hurt is like carrying a heavy backpack everywhere—it wears you out. Forgiveness is how we set the backpack down.

Joseph knew what hurt felt like. His brothers sold him as a slave! Years later, when Joseph was powerful in Egypt and his brothers needed help, he could have paid them back. But Joseph forgave them. He said, "God used it for good," and he cared for them. Joseph didn't pretend it wasn't wrong. He chose to forgive and let God heal his heart.

Forgiving doesn't mean what happened was okay. It means you give your anger to God and choose not to get even. Jesus forgave us, even when it cost Him everything on the cross. When we remember His forgiveness, we can forgive others—even when it's hard.

Your heart will feel lighter when you let go and let God work.

Let's Think About It

» Is there someone you need to forgive?

» What could you say or do to begin forgiving them?

A Simple Prayer

Jesus, thank You for forgiving me. Help me to forgive others like You forgive me. Amen.

Your Weekly Challenge

Write a short note (or say it in person) to someone you're forgiving: "I forgive you." If that's not possible, tell God you forgive them and pray for them.

Week 7: Ready to Serve

Bible Verse

"For even the Son of Man came not to be served but to serve," — Mark 10:45 (ESV)

The Big Idea

Imagine the King of everything washing dirty feet. That's what Jesus did for His friends. On the night before the cross, He wrapped a towel around His waist and washed the disciples' feet—something only servants did. Jesus showed that real greatness looks like serving.

Serving means looking for needs and meeting them: clearing the table without being asked, helping a sibling with homework, or picking up trash that no one else noticed. It's not about applause; it's about love. Jesus, the greatest of all, chose the lowest place. When we serve, we become more like Him.

Think of a team—everyone has a role. In God's family, we use our gifts to help each other win. Some people teach, some encourage, some fix things, some cook, some lead songs. All of it matters. When we serve with joy, people see Jesus in us.

Be ready with a towel-heart: quick to help, happy to love.

Let's Think About It

» What's one way you can serve at home this week?

» What's a small need at school you could meet?

A Simple Prayer

Lord Jesus, You served me first. Give me eyes to see needs and a heart eager to help. Amen.

Your Weekly Challenge

Choose one person to secretly serve every day this week—then do it with a smile.

Week 8: Thankful Hearts

Bible Verse

"Oh give thanks to the LORD, for he is good," — Psalm 107:1 (ESV)

The Big Idea

Saying "thank you" is more than good manners—it's a way to remember God's goodness. Jesus once healed ten men with leprosy, a terrible skin disease. They all ran off happy, but only one came back to say thank you. Jesus noticed.

Gratitude changes how we see things. Instead of focusing on what we don't have, we start seeing what God has already given—family, friends, food, sunshine, laughter, and His never-ending love. When you thank God, you're saying, "I see Your goodness, and I'm glad."

It's easy to complain about chores or homework, but what if we thanked God for a home to clean, a mind to learn, and teachers who care? Thanksgiving turns ordinary days into worship. The more we thank God, the more joy grows in our hearts.

Don't be like the nine who forgot—be the one who returns to praise.

Let's Think About It

» What are three things you're thankful for today?

» Who is someone you could thank in person?

A Simple Prayer

Good Father, You are so good. Thank You for blessings big and small. Teach me a thankful heart. Amen.

Your Weekly Challenge

Start a "gratitude jar." Each day, write one thing you're thankful for on a slip of paper and drop it in.

Week 9: Shine Your Light

Bible Verse

"Let your light shine before others," —
Matthew 5:16 (ESV)

The Big Idea

Have you ever used a flashlight in a dark room? One little light makes a big difference! Jesus said we are like lights in the world. When we live God's way—loving others, telling the truth, showing kindness—people see a little bit of God's light through us.

In the Bible, Queen Esther shined her light by being brave. She spoke up to save her people, even when it was risky. She didn't hide. She used the place God put her to do good. You have places too—your school, team, neighborhood—where your light can shine.

Shining your light doesn't mean being loud or perfect. It means being faithful in small things: including someone left out, standing up for what's right, saying sorry when you mess up, and sharing why you have hope in Jesus. When you do, others no-tice—and God gets the glory.

Don't hide your light. The world needs it.

Let's Think About It

» Where is one place you can shine for Jesus this week?

» What action will help your light shine there?

A Simple Prayer

Jesus, help me shine Your light with love and cour-age. Use me to point others to You. Amen.

Your Weekly Challenge

Choose one "shine moment" each day—like encour-aging a classmate or telling the truth even when it's hard.

Week 10: Ask for Wisdom

Bible Verse

"If any of you lacks wisdom, let him ask God," — James 1:5 (ESV)

The Big Idea

Have you ever wished for a superpower to make the right choice every time? God offers something even better: wisdom. When Solomon became king, he could have asked God for riches or power. Instead, he asked for wisdom to lead well. God loved that request and gave it generously.

Wisdom isn't just knowing a lot; it's knowing how to use what you know to honor God. It helps you choose friends, use your words well, handle anger, and decide what to do when no one is watching. The best part? God promises to give wisdom when we ask in faith.

How do we grow in wisdom? Pray. Read God's Word. Listen to wise adults. Think before you act. Ask, "What choice would please God?" Wisdom is like a light on the path that helps you not trip.

You don't have to guess your way through life. Ask God—and watch Him guide you.

Let's Think About It

» What is one choice you need wisdom for right now?

» Who is a wise person you can talk to this week?

A Simple Prayer

God, I need Your wisdom. Please guide my choices and help me live in a way that honors You. Amen.

Your Weekly Challenge

Before making a decision each day, pause and pray: "Lord, give me wisdom." Then choose with courage.

Week 11: Be a Peacemaker

Bible Verse

"If possible, so far as it depends on you, live peaceably with all." — Romans 12:18 (ESV)

The Big Idea

Arguments happen—about games, turns, or who's right. But God calls us to be peacemakers. Long ago, Abraham's family and his nephew Lot's family had too many animals for the same land. Their herders started arguing. Abraham chose peace. He let Lot pick the land first, even if it meant Abraham got the less "nice" side. God took care of Abraham because he trusted God more than he fought for stuff.

Being a peacemaker doesn't mean ignoring problems. It means handling them with gentleness and fairness. You can use calm words, listen well, say sorry first, and look for win-win solutions. Sometimes peace means walking away from a fight or choosing not to get the last word.

Jesus said peacemakers are blessed. When we choose peace, we look like God's children—bringing calm where there's conflict and love where there's tension.

Let's Think About It

» Where is there a conflict you can bring peace to?

» What peaceful words could you say this week?

A Simple Prayer

Lord, help me be a peacemaker. Give me calm words, a soft heart, and courage to do what's right. Amen.

Your Weekly Challenge

When a disagreement pops up, try this: pause, breathe, listen, and then speak gently. Aim for peace.

Week 12: Never Alone

Bible Verse

"I will never leave you nor forsake you."
— Hebrews 13:5 (ESV)

The Big Idea

Do you ever feel left out or lonely? God promises something amazing: He will never leave you. Shadrach, Meshach, and Abednego knew this when they refused to worship a statue. The king threw them into a fiery furnace—but God was with them. A fourth person appeared in the fire, and they came out without even the smell of smoke!

You might not face a furnace, but you will face hard days—a move to a new school, a sick family member, or friends who don't include you. In those moments, remember: God is with you in the fire and in the quiet. His presence is our comfort and courage.

When you feel alone, talk to God. Read His promises. Reach out to a trusted adult. God often shows His presence through His people. You are never really by yourself—your faithful God is right there.

Let's Think About It

» When do you feel most alone?

» What helps you remember that God is with you?

A Simple Prayer

God, thank You for being with me always. Help me feel Your presence and trust Your promises. Amen.

Your Weekly Challenge

Choose a verse about God's presence, write it on a card, and keep it where you'll see it every day.

Week 13: Do Your Best

Bible Verse

"Whatever you do, work heartily, as for the Lord" — Colossians 3:23 (ESV)

The Big Idea

Have you ever felt like cutting corners on chores or homework? Nehemiah didn't. When he heard Jerusalem's walls were broken, he prayed, planned, and got to work. Even when enemies mocked and tried to stop them, the people kept building—with a tool in one hand and protection in the other—until the wall was finished.

Working "as for the Lord" means doing your best because you love God, not just to impress people. Whether it's practicing piano, studying spelling, or helping at home, your effort is worship. God sees the small things and smiles when you use your gifts with a good attitude.

Doing your best doesn't mean being perfect. It means being faithful—showing up, trying hard, and not giving up when it's tough. God strengthens you to keep going, and He uses your work to bless others.

Let's Think About It

» What task do you need to give your best effort this week?

» How can you turn that task into worship to God?

A Simple Prayer

Lord, help me work with a happy heart and do my best for You in everything. Amen.

Your Weekly Challenge

Pick one task you usually rush. Slow down, make a plan, and do it heartily—then thank God when it's done.

Week 14: Walk in Integrity

Bible Verse

"Whoever walks in integrity walks securely," — Proverbs 10:9 (ESV)

The Big Idea

Integrity means being the same person in the dark as you are in the light—honest, faithful, and trustworthy. Daniel showed integrity when he refused to eat the king's food that would break God's law. He asked for vegetables and water instead and trusted God. God honored his choice, and Daniel became known for wisdom and honesty.

Integrity shows up in school when you don't peek at someone's answers, at home when you tell the truth about a broken vase, and online when you choose what's good. It's not always easy—sometimes being honest feels risky. But when you walk in integrity, you walk "securely," without the fear of getting caught or tangled in lies.

God sees your heart. He helps you choose what's right and forgives you when you mess up. Each honest choice builds a strong foundation for your life—step by step.

Let's Think About It

» Where do you need to choose honesty this week?

» Who can help you stay accountable?

A Simple Prayer

God, make my heart true. Help me walk in integrity in small things and big things. Amen.

Your Weekly Challenge

Tell the truth even if it's hard—then make it right if needed. Notice the peace that follows.

Week 15: Friends Who Stick

Bible Verse

"A friend loves at all times," — Proverbs 17:17 (ESV)

The Big Idea

Great friends are a gift! Think about David and Jonathan. Jonathan was the king's son, but he loved David like a brother. Even when his dad grew jealous of David, Jonathan protected his friend. He encouraged David, made promises before God, and stayed loyal. That's what real friendship looks like.

A good friend: listens, tells the truth kindly, forgives, includes others, and cheers you on. A not-so-good friend: gossips, pressures you to do wrong, or disappears when things get tough. God wants us to be the first kind of friend—and choose friends who help us follow Him.

Friendship takes effort. You have to show up, share, say sorry, and work through disagreements. But it's worth it! When friends "stick," they help each other grow strong in faith and joy.

Be the kind of friend you want to have—and pray for friends who love Jesus too.

Let's Think About It

» What makes someone a true friend?

» How can you be a better friend to someone this week?

A Simple Prayer

Jesus, thank You for friends. Teach me to love like You and be a faithful, kind friend. Amen.

Your Weekly Challenge

Write or tell one friend why you're thankful for them—and do one thing to encourage them this week.

Week 16: Better to Obey

Bible Verse

"Behold, to obey is better than sacrifice, and to listen than the fat of rams." — 1 Samuel 15:22 (ESV)

The Big Idea

Have you ever heard, "Please do it the first time"? Obedience isn't just about following rules—it's about trusting the one who gives them. In the Bible, King Saul disobeyed God. He did most of what God said but kept some things back because he thought his way was better. God sent Samuel to tell Saul that God cares more about obedience than fancy gifts. That's when Samuel said, "To obey is better than sacrifice."

Jonah learned this too. God told him to go to Nineveh, but Jonah ran the opposite way. A big storm and an even bigger fish changed his mind! When Jonah finally obeyed, God used him to help a whole city turn back to God. Obedience brings blessing—not because we earn God's love, but because we walk in His wise path.

Sometimes obedience is hard—like telling the truth when it's scary, turning off a game when your parents ask, or choosing not to join in gossip. But God's instructions are for our good. When we obey, we say, "God, I trust You."

Let's Think About It

» What's one instruction from God (or from your parents) you've been ignoring?

» How could trusting God help you obey with a good attitude?

A Simple Prayer

Lord, help me listen and obey. I trust that Your way is best. Give me a willing heart. Amen.

Your Weekly Challenge

Pick one area to "obey the first time." Tell a parent what you're choosing, and ask them to notice your progress.

Week 17: Choose Humility

Bible Verse

"Do nothing from selfish ambition or conceit, but in humility count others more significant than yourselves." — Philippians 2:3 (ESV)

The Big Idea

Humility is not thinking you're "less" but thinking of yourself less. The Bible says Jesus—God the Son—left heaven's glory to come as a servant. He washed His disciples' feet, welcomed kids, healed the hurting, and gave His life on the cross. That's the greatest picture of humility the world has ever seen.

Jesus also told a story about two men who went to the temple to pray. One bragged about himself. The other, a tax collector, knew he needed God's mercy. Jesus said the humble man went home right with God. God lifts up the humble!

At school, humility looks like letting someone else go first, sharing the spotlight, listening more than talking, and admitting when you're wrong. It's saying, "How can I help?" instead of, "Look at me!" Humility doesn't make you weak—it makes you more like Jesus.

Let's Think About It

» Where can you choose to put someone else first this week?

» What's one area where you need to say, "I'm sorry"?

A Simple Prayer

Jesus, You humbled Yourself for me. Help me be humble and put others first. Amen.

Your Weekly Challenge

Each day, quietly do one "others first" act—let someone choose the game, give the bigger slice, or celebrate a friend's win.

Week 18: Waiting Well

Bible Verse

"Wait for the LORD; be strong, and let your heart take courage; wait for the LORD!" — Psalm 27:14 (ESV)

The Big Idea

Waiting is hard—waiting for summer break, for your turn, or for an answer to prayer. Simeon and Anna knew all about waiting. God promised Simeon he would see the Savior before he died. He waited year after year. One day, Mary and Joseph brought baby Jesus to the temple, and the Holy Spirit told Simeon, "This is Him!" Simeon took Jesus in his arms and praised God. Anna, an elderly woman who worshiped and prayed daily, also saw Jesus and told others the good news.

Waiting well doesn't mean doing nothing. It means trusting God's timing, praying, staying faithful, and doing the next right thing. Joseph waited in prison before becoming a leader. David waited years before becoming king. While they waited, God shaped their hearts.

When you feel impatient, remember that God sees the whole picture. He's never late. He uses waiting to grow courage, patience, and faith in us.

Let's Think About It

» What are you waiting for right now?

» How can you trust God and "do the next right thing" while you wait?

A Simple Prayer

God, help me wait with courage and trust. Use this time to grow my heart. Amen.

Your Weekly Challenge

Create a "waiting plan": each time you feel impatient, pray one sentence and do one small helpful task.

Week 19: Cheerful Giving

Bible Verse

"Each one must give as he has decided in his heart, not reluctantly or under compulsion, for God loves a cheerful giver." — 2 Corinthians 9:7 (ESV)

The Big Idea

Jesus once sat by the temple offering box and watched people give. Rich people gave large amounts. Then a poor widow came and dropped in two tiny coins. Jesus told His disciples she had given more than everyone else—because she gave all she had, with a willing heart. God sees the heart behind the gift.

Generosity isn't about how much; it's about how joyful and loving you are when you give. You can give time (help a sibling), talents (draw a card for someone), and treasure (share your allowance). When you give cheerfully, you remember that everything you have is from God, and you get to be part of His work.

Generosity spreads joy. It blesses others, grows your faith, and reflects God's generous heart. Jesus gave us the greatest gift—Himself. When we give, we become more like Him.

Let's Think About It

» What can you give this week—time, talent, or treasure?

» How does remembering God's gifts to you make giving easier?

A Simple Prayer

Generous God, thank You for all You've given me. Make my heart cheerful and my hands open. Amen.

Your Weekly Challenge

Choose one person or cause to bless this week. Plan it, give it, and thank God for the chance to share.

Week 20: Words That Build

Bible Verse

"Let no corrupting talk come out of your mouths, but only such as is good for building up... that it may give grace to those who hear." — Ephesians 4:29 (ESV)

The Big Idea

Words are powerful—like bricks that build or wrecking balls that destroy. With your mouth, you can encourage, tell the truth, and praise God; or you can gossip, complain, and hurt. James compares the tongue to a small spark that can set a forest on fire. That's why God tells us to speak words that build others up.

Think of Barnabas in the book of Acts. His name means "son of encouragement." He encouraged new believers, defended Paul when others were unsure, and helped the church grow strong. Your words can do that too!

At school, building words sound like, "Great job," "I'm proud of you," "I forgive you," and "Can I help?" When you feel angry, pause before you speak. Ask, "Will these words give grace?" If not, choose different ones. God can help you turn hurtful words into helpful ones.

Let's Think About It

» What's a common phrase you say that needs to change?

» Who needs encouragement from you today?

A Simple Prayer

Lord, set a guard over my mouth. Help my words give grace and build others up. Amen.

Your Weekly Challenge

Keep a "word tally" for one day. For every encouraging word, draw a smiley. For every unkind word, a dot. Aim for more smiles!

Week 21: Strong on the Inside

Bible Verse

"Whoever is slow to anger is better than the mighty, and he who rules his spirit than he who takes a city." — Proverbs 16:32 (ESV)

The Big Idea

Self-control is like having strong "inside muscles." David showed self-control when King Saul hunted him. Twice, David had a chance to get even—once in a cave and once in a camp—yet he refused to harm Saul. David trusted God to handle justice. He ruled his spirit instead of letting anger rule him.

Self-control helps you pause before yelling, turn off a device when it's time, and stop after one cookie. It doesn't mean you never feel big emotions—it means you choose wise actions even when feelings are loud. God's Spirit grows self-control in us like fruit on a tree.

Ask God for help in the moment: "Lord, help me slow down." Breathe, count to ten, and remember what's true. Strong on the inside is better than strong on the outside.

Let's Think About It

» What situation makes it hard for you to show self-control?

» What is one plan you can use next time it happens?

A Simple Prayer

God, help me rule my spirit. Give me patience and strength to choose what's right. Amen.

Your Weekly Challenge

Pick one area to practice self-control (screens, sweets, or speech). Set a simple limit and stick to it all week.

Week 22: Hope in the Storm

Bible Verse

"May the God of hope fill you with all joy and peace in believing... so that by the power of the Holy Spirit you may abound in hope." — Romans 15:13 (ESV)

The Big Idea

One night, Jesus' disciples were on a boat when a fierce storm hit. Waves crashed, wind howled—and Jesus slept! Terrified, they woke Him. Jesus stood, spoke to the wind and waves, and everything grew calm. The disciples were amazed. "Who is this?" They saw that Jesus is Lord over storms.

Life has storms too—bad news, tough friendships, or changes you didn't choose. Hope isn't pretending storms aren't scary. Hope is trusting that Jesus is in the boat with you and has power to bring peace. He may calm the storm around you or the storm inside you—but He never leaves you.

When fear rises, remember who Jesus is. Pray, "Lord, speak Your peace." Read His promises. Talk to someone who loves Jesus. Hope grows when we focus on Him.

Let's Think About It

» What storm are you facing right now?

» What promise of God helps you have hope?

A Simple Prayer

Jesus, You are stronger than every storm. Fill me with Your peace and hope. Amen.

Your Weekly Challenge

Teach someone a "storm prayer"—a short sentence like, "Jesus, bring Your peace"—and use it together this week.

Week 23: The Good Shepherd

Bible Verse

"The LORD is my shepherd; I shall not want." — Psalm 23:1 (ESV)

The Big Idea

Sheep aren't very good at finding their way. They need a shepherd to guide, protect, and provide. Jesus told a story about a shepherd who had 100 sheep. When one got lost, he left the 99 to find it. When he found the sheep, he joyfully carried it home. That's God's heart for you.

God leads you beside "still waters" when He gives peace. He guides you on "right paths" through His Word. He protects you in scary valleys and celebrates when you come back after you've wandered. With God as your Shepherd, you have what you truly need—His presence, guidance, and care.

When you feel lost, call out to Him. When you don't know which way to go, ask Him to lead. He knows your name and loves you more than you can imagine.

Let's Think About It

» Where do you need God's guidance right now?

» How can you follow the Shepherd's voice this week?

A Simple Prayer

Good Shepherd, lead me today. Help me hear Your voice and follow You closely. Amen.

Your Weekly Challenge

Memorize Psalm 23:1. Say it each morning and night as a reminder of God's care.

Week 24: Honor at Home

Bible Verse

"Honor your father and your mother, that your days may be long in the land that the LORD your God is giving you."
— Exodus 20:12 (ESV)

The Big Idea

Honoring parents means treating them with respect—listening, obeying, thanking, and speaking kindly. When Jesus was twelve, He amazed teachers in the temple. But after that, He went home to Nazareth and "was submissive" to Mary and Joseph. The Son of God honored His earthly parents!

Honoring doesn't mean parents are perfect. It means recognizing the role God gave them to love, teach, and protect you. When you honor them, you honor God. You can disagree respectfully, ask questions kindly, and obey even when you'd rather not. God promises blessing with this command.

Honor shows up in little choices: putting your dish away, doing chores without grumbling, answering with "Yes, Mom/Dad," and saying "Thanks." Little honors make a big difference.

Let's Think About It

» What's one way you can honor your parents today?

» How can you respond respectfully even when you feel frustrated?

A Simple Prayer

Father, help me honor my parents with my words and actions. Give me a respectful, thankful heart. Amen.

Your Weekly Challenge

Do one extra helpful task each day this week without being asked. Tell no one—let it be your gift.

Week 25: Good News to Share

Bible Verse

"Go into all the world and proclaim the gospel to the whole creation." — Mark 16:15 (ESV)

The Big Idea

Philip was walking down a desert road when God led him to a chariot. Inside was a man from Ethiopia reading Isaiah but not understanding it. Philip hopped in, explained how the prophecy pointed to Jesus, and the man believed and was baptized. Philip was ready to share the good news!

The gospel is the best news: Jesus died for our sins, rose again, and invites us into God's family by faith. Sharing doesn't mean giving a long speech. It can be as simple as telling your story, inviting a friend to church, praying for someone, or explaining why you have hope in Jesus.

God places you in the perfect spots—your school, team, and neighborhood. Ask Him for courage and love. The Holy Spirit opens hearts; we just open our mouths.

Let's Think About It

» Who is one person you can pray for and encourage toward Jesus?

» What is one sentence you could share about what Jesus means to you?

A Simple Prayer

Lord, make me brave and kind as I share about You. Give me the right words at the right time. Amen.

Your Weekly Challenge

Write your 3-point story: "Before Jesus," "How I met Jesus," "What's different now." Share it with a trusted friend or family member.

Week 26: Stand Out, Don't Blend In

Bible Verse

"Do not be conformed to this world, but be transformed by the renewal of your mind..." — Romans 12:2 (ESV)

The Big Idea

Sometimes it feels easier to blend in—laugh at the joke, follow the crowd, or hide your faith. Noah didn't blend in. When the world was full of wickedness, God told Noah to build an ark. People probably laughed. It took a long time. Yet Noah obeyed. When the flood came, Noah and his family were safe because he listened to God, not the crowd.

Standing out means living God's way even when it's unpopular: telling the truth, choosing clean entertainment, including the lonely, and honoring God with your words. Your mind is "renewed" as you read Scripture and think about what's true and good. God helps you know His will and gives you strength to live it.

You don't stand out alone—God stands with you.

Let's Think About It

» Where do you feel pressure to blend in?

» What's one way you can stand for what's right this week?

A Simple Prayer

God, transform my thoughts and choices. Give me courage to live Your way, even when it's hard. Amen.

Your Weekly Challenge

Choose one "stand-out" action—like changing a playlist, stepping away from gossip, or inviting someone in—and do it.

Week 27: Speak, Lord

Bible Verse

"And the LORD came and stood, calling as at other times, 'Samuel! Samuel!' And Samuel said, 'Speak, for your servant hears.'" — 1 Samuel 3:10 (ESV)

The Big Idea

Samuel was a boy serving in the temple when God called his name at night. He thought it was Eli, the priest, and ran to him—three times! Eli finally understood and told Samuel to say, "Speak, for your servant hears." Samuel listened, and God began speaking to him regularly.

God speaks to us today through His Word, the Bible. He can also guide our hearts by His Spirit, through wise people, and through the peace He gives. Listening to God means making space to be quiet, reading Scripture, and being ready to obey what He shows you.

You can create "listening moments": a few minutes in the morning or before bed, asking God to teach you. Keep a notebook for verses and thoughts. Like Samuel, answer, "Speak, Lord. I'm listening."

Let's Think About It

» When can you create a quiet "listening time" each day?

» What verse has God used to speak to you recently?

A Simple Prayer

Lord, I'm listening. Speak through Your Word and help me obey what You say. Amen.

Your Weekly Challenge

Set a 5-minute "quiet time" each day. Read a Psalm or a Gospel story and write one short sentence you learned.

Week 28: You're Not Too Young

Bible Verse

"Let no one despise you for your youth, but set the believers an example in speech, in conduct, in love, in faith, in purity." — 1 Timothy 4:12 (ESV)

The Big Idea

A huge crowd was hungry, and the disciples didn't know what to do. A boy offered his lunch—five loaves and two fish. Jesus took the small gift, gave thanks, and multiplied it to feed thousands, with baskets left over! God loves using kids in His big plans.

You're not too young to make a difference. You can lead by example—kind words, good choices, loving actions, strong faith, and a pure heart. Your small offering—time, talent, or treasure—becomes big in Jesus' hands.

Don't wait to be older to follow God bravely. Bring what you have to Jesus today, and watch Him do more than you imagined.

Let's Think About It

» What "loaves and fish" can you offer Jesus this week?

» Where can you set a good example for others?

A Simple Prayer

Jesus, here's my small lunch—my time, gifts, and heart. Use me for Your glory. Amen.

Your Weekly Challenge

Pick one area from 1 Timothy 4:12 and focus on it all week—speech, conduct, love, faith, or purity.

Week 29: Care for God's World

Bible Verse

"The LORD God took the man and put him in the garden of Eden to work it and keep it." — Genesis 2:15 (ESV)

The Big Idea

From the beginning, God asked people to care for His world. That means we are stewards—managers of what belongs to God. The earth, animals, water, trees, and even your own body are gifts to "work and keep."

Noah cared for animals on the ark. Farmers plant and harvest. Families recycle, pick up trash, and use resources wisely. Caring for creation shows respect to the Creator. It's not about being perfect; it's about being faithful—small, daily choices that protect and enjoy God's gifts.

You can turn off lights, save water, plant something, reuse items, and thank God for sunsets and starry skies. When we care for creation, we also care for people, because a clean, healthy world blesses everyone.

Let's Think About It

» What is one way you can "work and keep" God's world this week?

» How can your family make a creation-care plan?

A Simple Prayer

Creator God, thank You for this beautiful world. Help me be a wise and joyful caretaker. Amen.

Your Weekly Challenge

Do a mini clean-up—your room, a yard, or a park area. Take before/after photos and thank God for the difference.

Week 30: Joy, No Matter What

Bible Verse

"Rejoice in the Lord always; again I will say, rejoice." — Philippians 4:4 (ESV)

The Big Idea

Paul and Silas were thrown into prison for telling people about Jesus. Their feet were in stocks, and it was midnight. What did they do? They prayed and sang hymns! Suddenly, an earthquake shook the prison, doors opened, and chains fell off. Their joy didn't depend on perfect circumstances—it came from the Lord.

Joy is deeper than a happy mood. It's a gladness rooted in who God is and what He's done. We can rejoice because Jesus loves us, forgives us, is with us, and is working for our good. Joy can live alongside tears and questions. It whispers, "God is faithful," even on hard days.

You can choose joy by thanking God, singing, remembering His promises, and sharing good news with others. Joy is contagious—spread it!

Let's Think About It

» What helps you choose joy when things are tough?

» What promise of God lifts your heart?

A Simple Prayer

God, fill my heart with Your joy. Help me rejoice in You, no matter what happens. Amen.

Your Weekly Challenge

Start each day with a "joy jumpstart": list three blessings, sing one worship song, and smile at three people.

Week 31: Escape Hatch!

Bible Verse

"No temptation has overtaken you that is not common to man. God is faithful, and he will not let you be tempted beyond your ability, but with the temptation he will also provide the way of escape, that you may be able to endure it." — 1 Corinthians 10:13 (ESV)

The Big Idea

Have you ever really wanted to do something you knew was wrong? Maybe peeking at a friend's test, sneaking extra screen time, or saying something mean to fit in. That's temptation—like a strong pull in the wrong direction. The Bible says everyone faces it. But here's good news: God always provides a "way of escape."

Jesus understands temptation. After fasting in the wilderness, the devil tempted Him three times—offering food, power, and a flashy rescue. Jesus answered each one with Scripture and chose God's way. He didn't argue with temptation; He spoke truth and stepped away.

Your "escape hatch" might look like:

» Praying a quick prayer: "Lord, help me."

» Walking away from the situation.

» Telling a trusted adult.

Think of it like a fire drill for your heart. You don't wait for the flames—you practice now so you're ready later. Temptation comes, but you don't have to fall for it. With God's help, you can choose what's right and feel the freedom of saying, "I did it God's way!"

Let's Think About It

» What temptation shows up most for you?

» What "escape plan" will you try next time?

A Simple Prayer

God, when I'm tempted, show me the way out. Give me strength to choose Your way. Amen.

Your Weekly Challenge

Pick one Bible verse to use as your "escape verse." Write it on a card and carry it with you.

Week 32: Heart Over Hype

Bible Verse

"But the LORD said to Samuel, 'Do not look on his appearance or on the height of his stature, because I have rejected him. For the LORD sees not as man sees: man looks on the outward appearance, but the LORD looks on the heart.'" — 1 Samuel 16:7 (ESV)

The Big Idea

It's easy to be impressed by what we see—cool clothes, high scores, a funny personality. When Samuel went to anoint the next king of Israel, he saw David's older brothers and thought, "Wow, they look kingly!" But God said no. He chose David, the youngest shepherd boy. Why? Because God looks at the heart.

At school, people might notice who's popular, fastest, or best at art. God notices kindness when no one's watching, honesty in small moments, and a heart that wants to please Him. David wasn't perfect, but he loved God and trusted Him. God used David's heart more than his height.

You don't have to chase all the hype. You can focus on your heart: choosing truth, helping others, forgiving quickly, and spending time with God. Build a strong inside world, and God will take care of the outside stuff.

Let's Think About It

» What do you think God sees and loves in your heart?

» How can you grow a God-pleasing heart this week?

A Simple Prayer

Lord, help me care more about my heart than my image. Shape my heart to look like Yours. Amen.

Your Weekly Challenge

Do one kind thing in secret each day this week—something only you and God know.

Week 33: Tell God Your Worries

Bible Verse

"casting all your anxieties on him, because he cares for you." — 1 Peter 5:7 (ESV)

The Big Idea

Worries can feel like buzzing bees in your brain—tests, friendships, health, or family stuff. God invites you to throw those worries onto Him because He truly cares. Hannah knew this. She was deeply sad because she had no child. She went to the temple and poured out her heart to God. Later, God answered her prayer with a son, Samuel.

Casting your anxiety isn't pretending your worries aren't real. It's choosing a new place to put them—into God's strong hands. You can talk to Him anywhere: on the bus, at recess, or in your room. Try this pattern: "God, I'm worried about _____. I give it to You. Help me trust You." Then breathe and remember He hears.

You can also write worries on paper and place them in a "God box," symbolizing giving them to Him. Share with a parent, pastor, or teacher too—God often comforts us through people who love us.

God's not annoyed by your worries. He is ready to carry them—and you.

Let's Think About It

» What's your biggest worry right now?

» Who is a trusted person you can talk to about it?

A Simple Prayer

Father, I give You my worries. Thank You for caring for me. Please give me Your peace. Amen.

Your Weekly Challenge

Start a worry-to-prayer list. Each time a worry pops up, write it down and turn it into a one-sentence prayer.

Week 34: Clean Slates

Bible Verse

"If we confess our sins, he is faithful and just to forgive us our sins and to cleanse us from all unrighteousness." — 1 John 1:9 (ESV)

The Big Idea

Have you ever tried to hide a mistake—like blaming the dog for a mess or deleting a browser tab fast? Hiding feels heavy. David tried to hide his sin after he made a big mistake. Then God sent the prophet Nathan to help David see the truth. David confessed and wrote Psalm 51, asking God to create a clean heart in him. God forgave him.

Confessing means agreeing with God about what you did—no excuses, no blaming. It might sound like, "God, I lied. I'm sorry. Please forgive me and help me tell the truth." Because of Jesus' death and resurrection, forgiveness is sure. God doesn't rub it in; He wipes it out.

It's also good to confess to someone you wronged and make it right—return what you took, fix what you broke, and rebuild trust. A clean slate feels like stepping into sunshine after a storm. God's mercy is bigger than your mess.

Let's Think About It

» Is there a sin you need to confess to God today?

» What step can you take to make things right with someone?

A Simple Prayer

Merciful God, I'm sorry for my sin. Please forgive me and make my heart clean. Help me do what's right. Amen.

Your Weekly Challenge

Do a "heart check" before bed: ask God to show you anything to confess, then receive His forgiveness.

Week 35: New Places, Same God

Bible Verse

"Have I not commanded you? Be strong and courageous. Do not be frightened, and do not be dismayed, for the LORD your God is with you wherever you go."
— Joshua 1:9 (ESV)

The Big Idea

New can be exciting—and scary. New grade, new team, new school, new bus route. Joshua knew the feeling. Moses had led God's people for years. Now it was Joshua's turn to lead them into the Promised Land. God told Joshua to be strong and courageous because He would be with him wherever he went.

Joshua didn't fight Jericho with giant muscles—he obeyed God's unusual plan: march around the city, blow trumpets, shout. God did the heavy lifting, and the walls fell. Courage isn't having zero fear; it's choosing to trust God in the face of fear.

You can be brave by remembering: same God, new place. Pray before you walk into the classroom. Ask God to help you be friendly and faithful. Try small courageous steps—say hello first, raise your hand, or try out for the team. God walks in with you.

Let's Think About It

» What "new" are you facing?

» What's one brave step you can take with God this week?

A Simple Prayer

God, thank You for going with me into new places. Make me strong and courageous. Amen.

Your Weekly Challenge

Before each new or scary moment, pause and whisper Joshua 1:9. Then step in with a smile.

Week 36: Suit Up!

Bible Verse

"Put on the whole armor of God, that you may be able to stand against the schemes of the devil." — Ephesians 6:11 (ESV)

The Big Idea

Every day is like stepping onto a field—you need the right gear. God gives "armor" for your heart and mind: the belt of truth, breastplate of righteousness, shoes of the gospel of peace, shield of faith, helmet of salvation, and the sword of the Spirit (God's Word).

Think of it this way:

» Belt of Truth: Tighten up with what's true, not rumors or lies.

» Breastplate of Righteousness: Protect your heart by choosing what's right.

» Shoes of Peace: Be ready to bring good news and calm, not drama.

» Shield of Faith: Block doubts and mean words

by trusting God.

» Helmet of Salvation: Remember you belong to Jesus—your mind is guarded.

» Sword of the Spirit: Answer temptations with Scripture like Jesus did.

When a classmate teases you, raise the shield of faith and the sword of Scripture. When you're tempted to cheat, fasten the belt of truth. When the hallway feels tense, wear shoes of peace and be the calm. God's armor fits you perfectly.

Let's Think About It

» Which piece of armor do you need most this week?

» What verse can be your "sword" in tough moments?

A Simple Prayer

Lord, help me put on Your armor today. Make me strong to stand and kind to love. Amen.

Your Weekly Challenge

Draw the armor of God and label each piece. Post it where you'll see it before school.

Week 37: More Than Enough

Bible Verse

"And my God will supply every need of yours according to his riches in glory in Christ Jesus." — Philippians 4:19 (ESV)

The Big Idea

Have you ever worried you didn't have enough—time, money, courage, or lunch? Elijah met a widow who had almost nothing: a handful of flour and a little oil. She was preparing one last meal for herself and her son. Elijah said, "Make me a small cake first," trusting God's promise. She obeyed, and God kept the flour and oil from running out until the famine ended.

God knows what you need—food, friends, wisdom, help—and He loves to provide. It may not be fancy or instant, but it will be enough. Sometimes He provides through parents, church, neighbors, unexpected kindness, or your own hard work.

This doesn't mean we get everything we want. Wants and needs are different. But God delights to meet needs and teach us to trust Him. When you feel "not enough," remember God's "more than enough."

Let's Think About It

» What do you need from God right now?

» How has God provided for you before?

A Simple Prayer

Provider God, You see my needs. Please supply what I lack and help me trust You. Amen.

Your Weekly Challenge

Start a "provision journal." Write down one way each day you see God provide—big or small.

Week 38: Open the Door

Bible Verse

"Contribute to the needs of the saints and seek to show hospitality." — Romans 12:13 (ESV)

The Big Idea

Hospitality means making space for others—welcoming, including, and sharing what you have. Abraham did this in a big way. Three visitors came by his tent, and he hurried to offer water, shade, and a feast. Those visitors were actually messengers from God, bringing a promise about a son!

You can show hospitality without a tent or a feast. Invite the new kid to sit with you. Make space in the game for someone who's always picked last. Share your art supplies. Offer your best seat. Use people's names and smile. Hospitality turns strangers into friends.

When we welcome others, we echo God's welcome to us in Jesus. He opened His life to us—now we open ours to others. A simple "Want to join?" can change someone's day.

Let's Think About It

» Who is one person you can welcome this week?

» What can you share to help someone feel at home?

A Simple Prayer

Jesus, thank You for welcoming me. Help me open my heart, hands, and space to others. Amen.

Your Weekly Challenge

Plan one act of hospitality: invite, include, or share—and follow through with joy.

Week 39: Little Things Matter

Bible Verse

"One who is faithful in a very little is also faithful in much, and one who is dishonest in a very little is also dishonest in much." — Luke 16:10 (ESV)

The Big Idea

Want to be trusted with big responsibilities? Start with the small ones. In Jesus' parable of the talents, a master gave money to three servants. Two used it wisely and doubled it. The master said, "Well done! You've been faithful over a little; I will set you over much." The third buried his talent and wasted the opportunity.

Faithfulness looks like finishing homework, feeding the dog, returning things you borrow, and telling the truth about tiny details. Those "little" choices are like training reps for your character. They build trust with God and people.

If you cut corners on small stuff, you're practicing being untrustworthy. But when you're faithful, doors open. God loves to multiply faithfulness.

Let's Think About It

» What small job can you do with excellence this week?

» Where do you need to stop cutting corners?

A Simple Prayer

God, help me be faithful in little things so I can honor You in big things too. Amen.

Your Weekly Challenge

Pick one small duty (bed, backpack, instrument practice) and track a perfect streak for seven days.

Week 40: Rest Is Worship

Bible Verse

"Come to me, all who labor and are heavy laden, and I will give you rest." —
Matthew 11:28 (ESV)

The Big Idea

Sometimes life feels like sprint-sprint-sprint—school, sports, lessons, chores, repeat. God built rest right into creation. After six days of making the world, He rested on the seventh day and blessed it. Rest isn't laziness; it's a gift that helps our bodies and hearts reset.

Jesus invites the tired and stressed to come to Him for rest. That might look like setting aside screens for quiet time, reading Scripture, taking a peaceful walk, or worshiping with your church family. Sabbath-type rest reminds us: God is God; we are not. We can stop and trust Him.

Rest also means saying "no" sometimes, leaving margin in your schedule, and going to bed on time. When you rest God's way, you refuel to love and serve better. Rest becomes worship when you use it to draw close to Him.

Let's Think About It

» What makes you feel the most "heavy laden"?

» How can you plan a simple, God-focused rest time this week?

A Simple Prayer

Jesus, I come to You tired. Give me Your rest and teach me to trust You with my time. Amen.

Your Weekly Challenge

Plan a mini-Sabbath: one hour of no homework, no chores, no screens—just Scripture, prayer, and something peaceful.

Week 41: Speak Up with Love

Bible Verse

"Open your mouth for the mute, for the rights of all who are destitute." —
Proverbs 31:8 (ESV)

The Big Idea

Have you seen someone teased, ignored, or pushed out of a game? God calls us to speak up for people who can't speak for themselves. Nathan did this with King David. After David sinned, Nathan told a story that helped David see his wrong. It took courage to tell the truth to a king! But Nathan cared more about what was right than about being comfortable.

Speaking up doesn't mean being rude. It means using caring, clear words at the right time. You might say, "That joke isn't kind," or "Let's include him," or tell a teacher when someone is being hurt. You can also encourage the person left out: "Want to join us?" Truth plus love makes a powerful team.

God gives courage to stand up, wisdom to speak gently, and compassion to notice. Your voice can be a shield for someone else.

Let's Think About It

» Where do you see someone who needs a defender?

» What loving words could you use to help?

A Simple Prayer

God, give me courage to speak up and a gentle heart to do it with love. Amen.

Your Weekly Challenge

Practice one sentence you can say when you see unkindness. Then use it if you need to this week.

Week 42: Second Chances

Bible Verse

"Then the word of the LORD came to Jonah the second time, saying," —
Jonah 3:1 (ESV)

The Big Idea

Everyone messes up. The question is, what happens next? Jonah ran away from God's assignment and ended up in a storm and a great fish's belly. After Jonah prayed, God rescued him—and then spoke to him again. "The word of the LORD came... the second time." God still had a plan, and Jonah got a second chance.

Second chances don't erase consequences, but they open doors to try again with God's help. Maybe you failed a test, lost your temper, or quit something too soon. Bring it to God. Ask forgiveness if needed. Then listen for His "second time" voice: "Let's try again."

God is patient. He uses our do-overs to grow humility and strength. Don't let shame freeze you. With God, you can get back up.

Let's Think About It

» Where do you need a second chance?

» What's one step you can take to start again with God?

A Simple Prayer

God, thank You for second chances. Help me get back up and follow You with a teachable heart. Amen.

Your Weekly Challenge

Pick one area to restart—study habit, kindness, or prayer time. Make a simple plan and begin today.

Week 43: The Secret of Contentment

Bible Verse

"Not that I am speaking of being in need, for I have learned in whatever situation I am to be content." —
Philippians 4:11 (ESV)

The Big Idea

Contentment means being thankful and satisfied with what God has given—whether it's a small slice of cake or the newest game console (or not!). Paul wrote about contentment while in prison. He said he learned to be content when he had a lot and when he had a little, because his strength came from Jesus.

Wanting isn't wrong, but when we think, "I'll only be happy if I get that," it steals joy. Contentment says, "God has given me enough for today." You can practice by celebrating friends' wins, enjoying what you already have, and remembering God's faithfulness.

Try swapping "I need" for "It would be nice, but I'm thankful either way." Contentment grows joy and peace, no matter what your stuff or schedule looks like.

Let's Think About It

» What do you often say "I need" about?

» What are three blessings you can enjoy today?

A Simple Prayer

Lord, teach me contentment. Help me find my joy in You, not in things. Amen.

Your Weekly Challenge

Choose one thing to pause (ads, toy videos, shopping apps) for a week, and thank God daily for what you have.

Week 44: Growing Good Fruit

Bible Verse

"But the fruit of the Spirit is love, joy, peace, patience, kindness, goodness, faithfulness, gentleness, self-control; against such things there is no law." — Galatians 5:22–23 (ESV)

The Big Idea

Imagine your life as a tree. What grows on it shows what's happening inside. When we stay close to Jesus, the Holy Spirit grows good fruit in us—love when it's hard, joy on rainy days, peace in chaos, patience in long lines, kindness to siblings, goodness in choices, faithfulness in commitments, gentleness in our tone, and self-control with our actions.

Jesus said, "I am the vine; you are the branches." Branches don't strain to grow fruit—they stay connected. You don't force fruit by trying super hard. You grow fruit by spending time with Jesus: reading Scripture, praying, worshiping, and obeying. Over time, others will taste and see God's goodness in your life.

Pick one fruit to focus on. Ask God to grow it. Look for little moments to practice—waiting your turn, speaking softly, keeping a promise. Little sprouts become big fruit.

Let's Think About It

» Which fruit of the Spirit do you most want to grow?

» What's one way you can stay "connected to the Vine" this week?

A Simple Prayer

Holy Spirit, grow Your fruit in me. Help me stay close to Jesus every day. Amen.

Your Weekly Challenge

Choose one fruit and set a daily goal. Track your "fruit moments" and celebrate progress with a family member.

Week 45: Love That Won't Let Go

Bible Verse

"For I am sure that neither death nor life, nor angels nor rulers, nor things present nor things to come, nor powers, nor height nor depth, nor anything else in all creation, will be able to separate us from the love of God in Christ Jesus our Lord." — Romans 8:38-39 (ESV)

The Big Idea

Have you heard the story of the prodigal son? A younger son took his inheritance early, left home, and wasted everything. When he finally came back, tired and sorry, his father ran to him, hugged him, and threw a welcome party. That's a picture of God's never-stopping love.

Paul says nothing can separate us from God's love—not scary things, not mistakes, not the future, not anything in all creation. When you feel like you've blown it, God's love reaches for you. When you feel alone, His love holds you. When life changes, His love stays.

This love doesn't make us careless. It makes us brave to confess, quick to forgive, and eager to love others. You are securely loved because of Jesus—every single day.

Let's Think About It

» When do you most need to remember God's unbreakable love?

» Who needs to hear about God's love from you this week?

A Simple Prayer

Father, thank You that nothing can separate me from Your love in Jesus. Help me live loved and love others well. Amen.

Your Weekly Challenge

Write Romans 8:38–39 on a sticky note and put it where you'll see it. Read it out loud each day and smile—you are loved!

Week 46: Scroll Smart

Bible Verse

"Finally, brothers, whatever is true, whatever is honorable, whatever is just, whatever is pure, whatever is lovely, whatever is commendable, if there is any excellence, if there is anything worthy of praise, think about these things." — *Philippians 4:8 (ESV)*

The Big Idea

Screens are everywhere—tablets, phones, TVs, computers. They help us learn, play, and connect. But not everything we see online is good for our hearts. God gives us a simple "filter" for our minds: true, honorable, just, pure, lovely, commendable. If it doesn't fit the list, it doesn't need space in your brain.

Daniel used a heart-filter in Babylon. Everyone around him ate the king's food and followed the crowd, but Daniel "resolved" not to defile himself. He made a wise plan, asked respectfully, and trusted God. God honored his choice and gave him wisdom and favor. You can make a plan too for your digital life.

Before you watch, play, or post, first pause and ask: "Does this help me think about what's true and good? Would I watch this with Jesus sitting next to me?" If a video is mean, if a chat gets gossipy, or if a game brings out your worst, you can hit "exit." Use tech for good—learn something new, encourage a friend, share a Bible verse, create something beautiful. Your mind matters to God. Fill it with things that point you to Him.

Let's Think About It

» What is one online thing you need to block, skip, or stop?

» What is one online thing that helps you grow closer to God?

A Simple Prayer

Lord, train my eyes and mind. Help me choose what is true and lovely, and say "no" to what isn't. Amen.

Your Weekly Challenge

Make a "Philippians 4:8 Filter" card. Before you tap, check the list. Replace one unhelpful screen habit with a life-giving one.

Week 47: Honest, Even When It's Hard

Bible Verse

"Lying lips are an abomination to the LORD, but those who act faithfully are his delight." — Proverbs 12:22 (ESV)

The Big Idea

Have you ever been tempted to say, "It wasn't me!" when you know it was? Or to stretch the truth to make yourself look better? Even small lies tangle us up. Zacchaeus knew about that. He had cheated people as a tax collector. Then Jesus came to his house and loved him. Zacchaeus stood up and said he would pay back what he took—four times as much—and give half his money to the poor. Meeting Jesus turned a cheater into a truth-teller.

Honesty shows up in daily life: admitting you broke the pencil, telling the real score, giving back the extra change, and not copying answers. It's scary sometimes because you might get in trouble. But honesty builds trust with others—and peace inside your heart. God delights in faithful, truthful choices.

If you've lied, don't hide. Confess it to God, then to the person you lied to. Make it right if you can. You might be surprised—people respect honesty, even when it's hard. Every time you choose truth, you make your character stronger.

Let's Think About It

» Where is it hardest for you to tell the truth?

» What's one step you can take to make something right?

A Simple Prayer

God, make me a truth-teller. Help me love honesty more than trying to look good. Amen.

Your Weekly Challenge

Ask a parent or teacher to keep you accountable. Tell them one honest confession this week—even a small one—and make it right.

Week 48: Team Jesus

Bible Verse

"Now you are the body of Christ and individually members of it." — 1 Corinthians 12:27 (ESV)

The Big Idea

Think about a soccer team. If everyone tries to be the goalie, the team won't do well. Each player has a role, and when everyone plays their part, the team wins. God's family is like that. The Bible says we're one body with many parts. Some of us are great encouragers, some are helpers, some are leaders, some are creative, some are prayer warriors. All are needed.

In the early church, believers shared what they had, prayed together, and helped anyone in need. Because they worked as a team, "the Lord added" more people every day. You can be a team player at church, at home, at school, and on your actual teams. That means showing up, doing your part, cheering others on, and not comparing your gifts to someone else's.

On a group project, use your strength and respect others' ideas. At home, do your chore without grumbling so the "family team" runs well. At church, welcome new kids and join in. When each "part" does its job, people see Jesus.

Let's Think About It

» What's one gift or role God has given you on "Team Jesus"?

» Where can you use that gift this week?

A Simple Prayer

Jesus, thank You for making me part of Your body. Help me play my part and value others' gifts. Amen.

Your Weekly Challenge

Choose one team you're on (family, class, church). Ask, "How can I help our team this week?" Then do it with joy.

Week 49: Gossip Stops With Me

Bible Verse

"For lack of wood the fire goes out, and where there is no whisperer, quarreling ceases." — Proverbs 26:20 (ESV)

The Big Idea

Gossip is like feeding sticks to a campfire—it keeps the drama burning. Whispered rumors, secrets shared without permission, and "Did you hear...?" can hurt people and wreck friendships. The Bible says if there's no whisperer, the quarrel goes out—no wood, no fire.

Remember when Miriam and Aaron spoke against Moses? God heard, and it caused big trouble. Our words aren't small to God. As His kids, we can be "firefighters," not "fire feeders." If someone starts gossiping, you can change the subject, speak up kindly ("Let's not talk about her when she's not here"), or walk away. If you've spread something, apologize and correct it: "I shouldn't have said that. It wasn't kind. I'm sorry."

Use your mouth for good fires: encouragement, prayer, gratitude. Imagine your school if everyone refused to gossip—the air would feel lighter!

Let's Think About It

» When are you most tempted to gossip—texts, lunch, bus rides?

» What's a sentence you can use to put the "fire" out?

A Simple Prayer

Lord, make me a peacemaker with my words. Help me stop gossip and spread kindness instead. Amen.

Your Weekly Challenge

Commit to a "no-gossip week." If you slip, make it right fast. Aim to speak three specific encouragements each day.

Week 50: First Things First

Bible Verse

"But seek first the kingdom of God and his righteousness, and all these things will be added to you." — Matthew 6:33 (ESV)

The Big Idea

Do you ever feel like your schedule is a stuffed backpack—homework, practice, music lessons, chores, friends? Jesus teaches us about priorities: put God first. When God is first, everything else finds its place. In Mary and Martha's home, Martha rushed around, stressed about serving. Mary sat at Jesus' feet and listened. Jesus said Mary chose the "good portion."

Putting God first doesn't mean you ignore homework or don't help with chores. It means you start with Him and honor Him in everything. Pray when you wake up. Read a short Bible passage before screens. Talk to God while you walk. Ask, "What would please You here?" When choices compete, choose what brings you closer to Jesus.

God knows you need food, clothes, and time for responsibilities. He promises to take care of you as you seek Him first. A God-first life is calmer, clearer, and stronger—because the most important thing is in the first place.

Let's Think About It

» What usually gets your "first" attention each day?

» What's one way you can give God your first this week?

A Simple Prayer

Jesus, be first in my heart, time, and choices. Help me seek Your kingdom in everything. Amen.

Your Weekly Challenge

Make a "first 5" plan: give God the first five minutes of your day—pray, read a few verses, and write one takeaway.

Week 51: When God Says "My Grace Is Enough"

Bible Verse

"But he said to me, 'My grace is sufficient for you, for my power is made perfect in weakness.'" — 2 Corinthians 12:9 (ESV)

The Big Idea

What happens when the prayer isn't answered the way you hoped? You don't make the team. The grade doesn't go up. The sickness lasts longer. Paul asked God three times to take away a "thorn," something really hard. God didn't remove it. Instead, He promised Paul something better for the moment: "My grace is enough, and My power shows up best in weakness."

This doesn't mean God never changes circumstances—He often does! But sometimes He strengthens us inside while the outside is still tough. Think of Jesus in the garden. He prayed honestly and then surrendered, "Your will be done." God carried Him through the cross to resurrection. When you face disappointment, you can be honest with God, receive His comfort, and look for how His power can shine in your weakness—patience, courage, compassion for others.

You are not failing if life is hard. You are not alone. God's grace meets you right where you are.

Let's Think About It

» Where do you need God's "enough" right now?

» How could God's power shine through your weakness this week?

A Simple Prayer

God, I wanted this to change—but I trust You. Give me grace that's enough and strength to keep going. Amen.

Your Weekly Challenge

When a disappointment hits, write a two-line prayer: "God, here's my hurt: ____. I receive Your grace." Share with a trusted adult.

Week 52: Run Your Race

Bible Verse

"Therefore, since we are surrounded by so great a cloud of witnesses, let us also lay aside every weight, and sin which clings so closely, and let us run with endurance the race that is set before us, looking to Jesus, the founder and perfecter of our faith," — Hebrews 12:1-2 (ESV)

The Big Idea

Imagine a big race day—crowds cheering, banners waving, and you at the starting line. The Bible says life with Jesus is like a race. You have a course marked out by God. Heroes of faith—Abraham, Moses, Esther, Ruth—are like fans in the stands cheering you on. To run well, you lay aside heavy weights (comparisons, grudges, distractions) and sins that trip you. And most of all, you keep your eyes on Jesus.

Peter walked on water when he looked at Jesus; he sank when he looked at the waves. In your daily life, "looking to Jesus" means reading His Word, talking to Him, and remembering His love. Some parts of the race are uphill (hard), some are downhill (fun), and some feel long. Endurance grows one step at a time—homework finished, kindness chosen, truth told, prayer prayed.

You've spent 52 weeks learning and growing. This isn't the finish line—it's your training! With Jesus running beside you, you can keep going. He started your faith, and He will finish it.

Let's Think About It

- What "weight" do you need to lay down to run lighter?

- What helps you keep your eyes on Jesus each day?

A Simple Prayer

Jesus, thank You for the race You've set before me. Help me run with endurance, eyes on You. Amen.

Your Weekly Challenge

Plan a "finish strong" celebration: review your favorite verses and challenges from this year, pick one to keep practicing, and thank God for the journey!

Discover More Books

Start each day with purpose, peace, and a deeper connection to God. Whether you're nurturing your own faith, guiding your children, or growing together as a family—this devotional series meets you right where life happens.

Collect the Whole Series

| Devotional for Dads | Devotional for Moms | Devotional for Kids |

Available at major online bookstores

Each book is a spiritual companion—designed to inspire, uplift, and transform. Together, they form a complete journey of faith for the whole family.

Don't wait—bring home the full set and let every day draw you closer to God, to each other, and to the life you were created for.

www.ingramcontent.com/pod-product-compliance
Lightning Source LLC
Chambersburg PA
CBHW031438120626
46545CB00006B/2461